597.34　　Owings, Lisa.
Owings　　Bull shark attack /

WITHDRAWN

22.95 6/0   102-359-734-9

Animal Attacks

BULL SHARK ATTACK

by Lisa Owings

BELLWETHER MEDIA · MINNEAPOLIS, MN

Are you ready to take it to the extreme? Torque books thrust you into the action-packed world of sports, vehicles, mystery, and adventure. These books may include dirt, smoke, fire, and dangerous stunts. WARNING: read at your own risk.

Library of Congress Cataloging-in-Publication Data

Owings, Lisa.
 Bull shark attack / by Lisa Owings.
    p. cm. -- (Torque: animal attacks)
 Includes bibliographical references and index.
 Summary: "Engaging images illustrate true bull shark attack stories and accompany survival tips. The combination of high-interest subject matter and light text is intended for students in grades 3 through 7" --Provided by publisher.
 ISBN 978-1-60014-787-6 (hardcover : alk. paper)
 1. Bull shark--Behavior--Juvenile literature. 2. Shark attacks--Juvenile literature. I. Title.
 QL638.95.C3O95 2013
 597.3'4--dc23
                                       2012011221

This edition first published in 2013 by Bellwether Media, Inc.

No part of this publication may be reproduced in whole or in part without written permission of the publisher. For information regarding permission, write to Bellwether Media, Inc., Attention: Permissions Department, 5357 Penn Avenue South, Minneapolis, MN 55419.

Text copyright © 2013 by Bellwether Media, Inc. TORQUE and associated logos are trademarks and/or registered trademarks of Bellwether Media, Inc.

SCHOLASTIC, CHILDREN'S PRESS, and associated logos are trademarks and/or registered trademarks of Scholastic Inc.

Printed in the United States of America, North Mankato, MN.

TABLE OF CONTENTS

Bone-Crunching Bull Sharks..... 4
Killer in the Water...................... 6
Fishing for Disaster 12
Prevent a Bull Shark Attack... 18
Survive a Bull Shark Attack... 20
Glossary... 22
To Learn More 23
Index 24

Bone-Crunching Bull Sharks

Bull sharks have earned their **reputation** as the most dangerous sharks in the world. They are violent **predators**. Teeth like sharp saw blades help them tear apart large animals. People who swim in the shallow waters where bull sharks hunt are easy **victims**. Meeting a bull shark is no day at the beach.

No One Is Safe

Bull sharks live in the ocean, but they can also swim up rivers. These nasty sharks have attacked dogs, people, and even horses in freshwater.

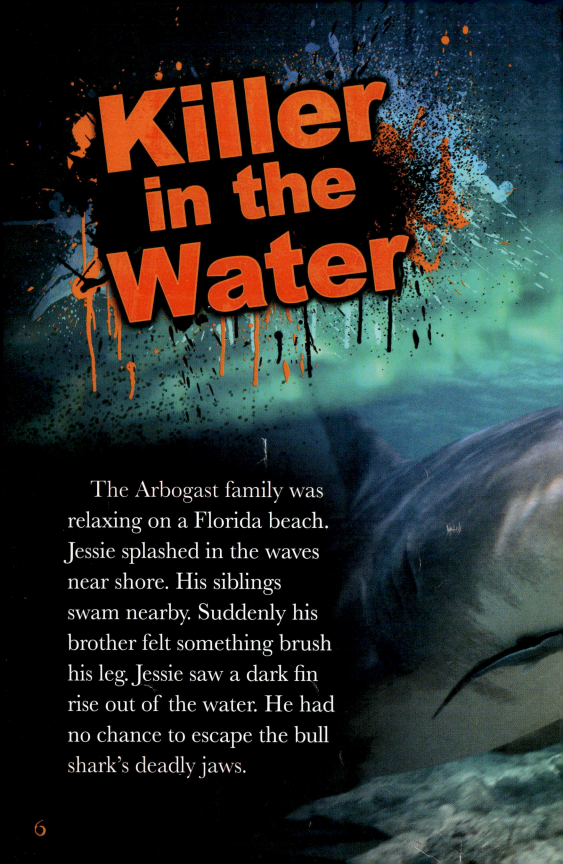

Killer in the Water

The Arbogast family was relaxing on a Florida beach. Jessie splashed in the waves near shore. His siblings swam nearby. Suddenly his brother felt something brush his leg. Jessie saw a dark fin rise out of the water. He had no chance to escape the bull shark's deadly jaws.

Tons of Teeth

Bull sharks have many rows of teeth. The teeth from back rows move forward to replace those that fall out or wear down.

The shark took a bite out of the eight-year-old's thigh. Then its rows of sharp teeth sliced into his arm. Jessie screamed, "He's got me!"

Vance Flosenzier heard his nephew's cry. He rushed into the blood-red water and gripped the shark's tail fin. Vance wrestled with the 200-pound (90-kilogram) fish. Then Jessie's arm was ripped from his body. The bleeding boy was carried to shore.

"I heard a scream, turned to the water, and saw a pool of blood."

—Vance Flosenzier

"I couldn't believe what was happening. It was just like a nightmare."
—Vance Flosenzier

the beach. Then he called 911. His wife Diana performed **CPR** on the wounded boy. Finally a helicopter came to rush Jessie to the hospital. A park ranger shot the shark. He forced open its jaws to save Jessie's arm. After hours of surgery, the arm was reattached. Jessie was clinging to life.

Jessie's Story

Jessie had lost most of his blood by the time help arrived. His heart had even stopped. His doctors saved his life, but he may never be able to walk again.

Jessie Arbogast

Fishing for Disaster

Craig Hutto and his brother Brian were fishing off the Florida coast. They caught fish after fish in waist-deep water. Suddenly Craig felt something bump into him. He couldn't see what it was through the **murky** water. Then powerful jaws crushed his leg. A bull shark dragged Craig deeper into the water.

Not the First Victim

Two days before Craig was attacked, a bull shark attacked and killed a girl at a nearby beach.

Brian swam after his brother. He grabbed Craig under the arms and began pulling him back to shore. The bull shark sank its teeth deeper into Craig's flesh. Craig struggled to keep his head above water. But his brother was winning the tug-of-war. They were getting closer to the beach.

Dragged into the Deep

Bull sharks often drag their prey underwater. Many attack victims drown before they bleed to death.

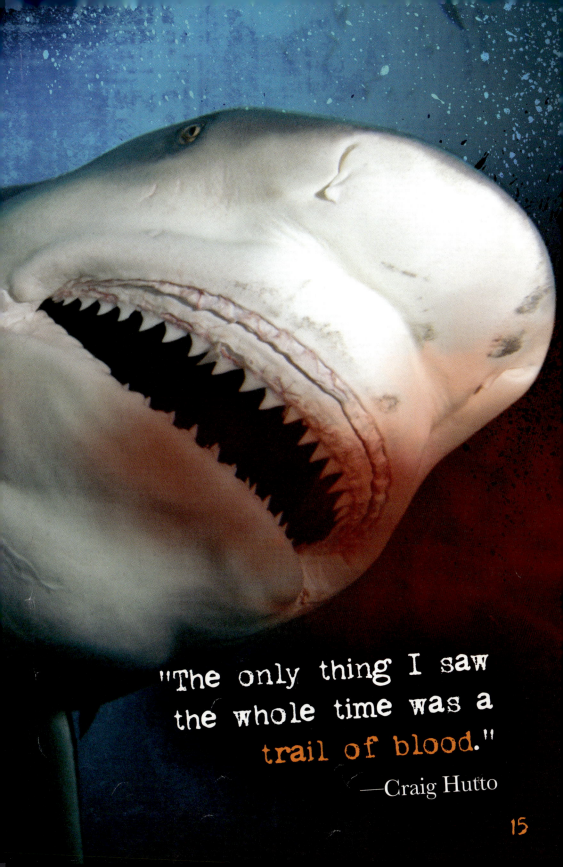

"The only thing I saw the whole time was a trail of blood."

—Craig Hutto

Craig tried to pry the shark's jaws off his leg. But its teeth were like knives. They shredded his hands. The shark was still holding on as the brothers reached shore. Brian punched the shark hard in the nose. It finally let go. Witnesses rushed to give Craig **first aid**. Doctors later had to remove Craig's leg, but his brother had saved his life.

Craig Hutto

Mechanical Man
Today, Craig is lucky to have two legs again. One of his legs is made of metal and controlled by a computer.

Prevent a Bull Shark Attack

Bull sharks attack people they think might be food. Swimmers often look like **prey**. The best way to prevent an attack is to avoid areas with bull sharks. Pay attention to signs that warn of bull shark sightings.

Never swim in the ocean alone or between **dusk** and **dawn**. This is when bull sharks are on the hunt. Stay out of murky water when you do swim. Be careful not to splash. It can make you look like injured prey.

Attracting Trouble

Do not wear jewelry or bright colors in the water. They can make you look like a shiny and colorful fish.

Feeding Frenzy

Stay away from bull sharks' favorite feeding areas. These include places where...

- **rivers empty into the sea**
- **people like to fish**
- **the sea floor slopes steeply downward**

Survive a Bull Shark Attack

Leave the water if you think you see or feel a bull shark. These sharks often head-butt their victims before attacking. If the shark attacks, do anything you can to get away. Hit or kick it in the nose, eyes, or **gills**. Then get out of the water. The bull shark will have to seek its supper somewhere else!

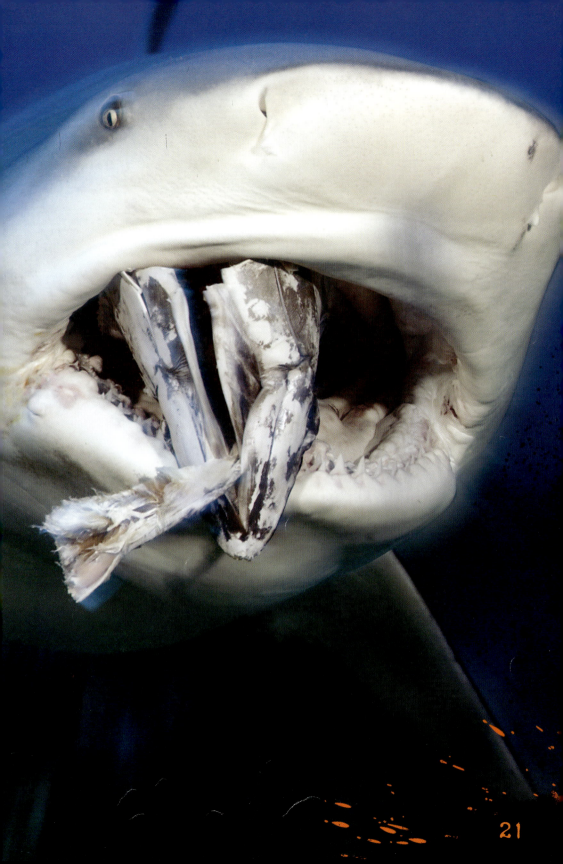

Glossary

CPR—an emergency medical procedure performed on a person whose heart and lungs have stopped working; CPR stands for cardiopulmonary resuscitation.

dawn—the beginning of the day when light first appears in the sky

dusk—the time of day just after the sun has set

first aid—emergency care given to an injured or sick person before medical help arrives

gills—sensitive organs near a shark's mouth; sharks and other fish breathe through gills.

murky—cloudy and dirty

predators—animals that hunt other animals for food

prey—animals that are hunted by other animals for food

reputation—what someone or something is known for doing

victims—people or animals that are hurt, killed, or made to suffer

To Learn More

At the Library

Discovery Channel. *Top 10 Deadliest Sharks*. Fort Washington, Pa.: Silver Dragon Books, 2010.

Dubowski, Cathy East. *Shark Attack!* New York, N.Y.: Dorling Kindersley, 2009.

Rake, Jody Sullivan. *Bull Shark*. Mankato, Minn.: Capstone Press, 2011.

On the Web

Learning more about bull sharks is as easy as 1, 2, 3.

1. Go to www.factsurfer.com.

2. Enter "bull sharks" into the search box.

3. Click the "Surf" button and you will see a list of related Web sites.

With factsurfer.com, finding more information is just a click away.

Index

Arbogast, Jessie, 6, 8, 11

attack prevention, 18, 19

CPR, 11

first aid, 17

Florida, 6, 12

Flosenzier, Diana, 11

Flosenzier, Vance, 8, 9, 10, 11

freshwater, 5, 19

Hutto, Brian, 12, 14, 17

Hutto, Craig, 12, 13, 14, 15, 17

jaws, 6, 11, 12, 17

prey, 14, 18

reputation, 4

survival, 20

teeth, 4, 7, 8, 14, 17